Magic in a Square

VINTAGE HANDKERCHIEFS
HOW & WHY TO USE THEM

CONCEIVED AND WRITTEN BY
BRUCE HELANDER

Essay by ANTHONY HADEN-GUEST   Essay by ELIZABETH SOBIESKI
Book Design by DAN ELLIS   Edited and coordinated by SUSAN HALL
Photography by TYLER SARGENT   Styling by CAMILA HELANDER SARGENT and CLAUDIA HELANDER
Original research KARENE TELESCA   Additional Magic by MIO
Rights and Reproductions by CAROL CALICCHIO

Left: One of Richard Merkin's paintings that will be in his May show at the Helander Gallery. The painting is entitled "Almedares: An Operetta." Above: Dapper Richard Merkin is ready for a night on the town after spending the day painting. His current favorite restaurant is Bernard, a bistro reminiscent of Paris's Left Bank.

Courtesy of *Vanity Fair*.

This book is dedicated to the memory of three amigos of mine, whose individual character and relentless commitment to stylish perfection were a remarkable influence on me.

In terms of understanding and appreciating personal style, painter **Richard Merkin** was the most influential man I ever met. As an eminent professor at the Rhode Island School of Design he was knowledgeable and charismatic, both as an artist and bon vivant. He taught me the inherent value of personal expression like no other, not just on canvas but also with personal style. He was an influential collector of eccentric objects and printed material, from vintage ephemera and photographs to magazine covers. I followed his inspiration by exploring collectables, which included pocket squares. Our friendship continued for over thirty years, during which time Richard became a contributing style editor at *GQ* and had a column in *Vanity Fair*, both with an enthusiastic following. Eventually, I had the good fortune to become his art dealer in Palm Beach and New York, where his continued presence enriched my life with high level creative energy.

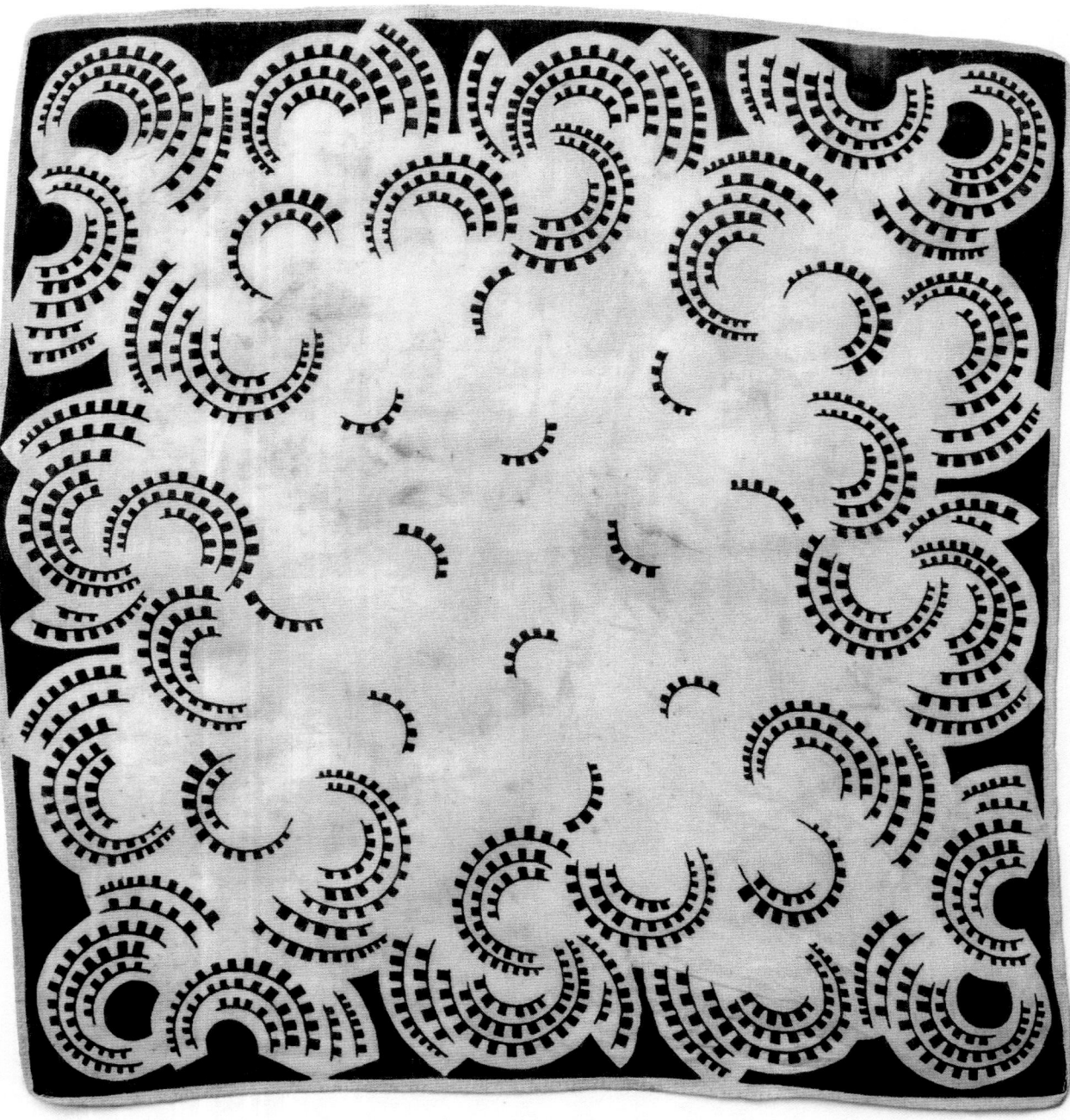

Professor Richard Merkin (left) and Bruce Helander (right; age 29), in black tie at a RISD reception honoring Robert Rauschenberg at the Whitney Museum of American Art.

Adjacent page: An original Art Deco masterpiece hank, absolutely perfect for a formal occasion.

Helander with Tom Wolfe, wearing a favorite hank, in Wolfe's spacious book-filled uptown townhouse in Manhattan. Helander book *Learning to See* is on the coffee table in the foreground.

Tom Wolfe, the celebrated writer and dean of New Journalism was a remarkable influence on me in appreciating and understanding what distinctive personal style meant. Arguably he was the best dressed man in Manhattan, but his legacy always will be his memorable manuscripts that incorporated a new way of telling a story with elegance and panache. From *The Electric Kool-Aid Acid Test* to *The Right Stuff*, Wolfe's novels portrayed contemporary history that revolutionized modern writing. He was an artist in his own right, often illustrating articles with delightful pen and ink drawings reflecting contemporary life. His long-running correspondence with me was a constant reminder about original idiosyncratic style, from a handsomely calligraphed envelope to a found handkerchief.

Richard Kaplan and Edwina Sandys.
Photograph by Michael Price. Taken at the launch party for *The Art Economist*,
Helander's magazine, at the New Museum in Manhattan.

Richard Kaplan was a great friend from Palm Beach and New York City. He was debonaire in the way that he was impeccably dressed and in what he had to say. He was the Chairman of the New York Foundation for the Arts as well as an accomplished architect. His loft in SoHo that he shared with his wife, artist Edwina Sandys, was a masterpiece of architecture and placement of furnishings that conveyed a distinguished sense of style, history and individuality. Richard always was a standout in a crowd with his dashing suits and charming intelligence. He was a man who inherently knew the value of a great pocket square and was never without one, which for me personally was welcome and ongoing encouragement to do the same.

Copyright © 2021 Bruce Helander
ISBN 978-1-66783-347-7

brucehelander.com   magicinasquare.com

No portion of this book may be reproduced without permission from the publisher. Brief quotes and illustrations are pre-approved for media reviews and articles. All rights reserved. No part of this book may be reproduced, stored in any retrieval system, or transmitted in any form, or by any means including but not limited to electronic, mechanical, photocopy, recording, or otherwise, without the written consent of the author and publisher.

Contents

13
INTRODUCTION
by Bruce Helander

15
PERFECT PLACEMENT AND FOLDING A HANK
by Bruce Helander

21
A HANKERING
by Bruce Helander

29
HANKY PANKY, THE LANGUAGE OF POCKET CLOTHS: LOST, BUT NOT FORGOTTEN. RIPE FOR REVIVAL?
by Anthony Haden-Guest

35
SQUARE-CUTS FOR STAR-SHAPES: CELEBRITIES AND THEIR POCKET SQUARES
by Elizabeth Sobieski

43
THE HELANDER COLLECTION

63
THE WEDDING DRESS

121
BEDSPREAD

An appropriate vintage pocket square in shades of chocolate brown to complement the Introduction, as the cloth design incorporates ten separate magical squares within a square. In the bottom right corner is a monogrammed initial "H" for Helander, of course!

Introduction

The Magic in a Square refers to the magical design within a pocket square and the magic a hank can create. Traditionally, a handkerchief was much larger and was used around the neck as a bandana. The pocket square came later, but for the purposes of this book, hanks, hankies, handkerchiefs, silk squares and poplin squares, are all interchangeable. My preference is the word 'hanky!'

However, there are no set rules, other than appreciating a good design. A gentleman or gentle-woman should not only match a pocket square with their outfit, but inventively contrast the material to act as a complementary accent piece. Just like an artist who creates a composition using the resources at hand, there are no set rules when it comes to choosing a square.

Theoretically, any fabric can be used but it should pass a simple test for the appropriateness of contrast, texture, color, design, weave, weight and fabric thickness, which is important for shaping. Generally speaking, the more formal the event, the less complicated the pocket square. Don't forget a pocket square can bring casual elegance and a stylish accent to an ensemble without a necktie. It's a good idea to start with a favorite hank that seems like a great companion to your clothes. You should not try to match colors too closely—particularly those shades in the tie that can make everything appear monochromatic. Practice makes perfect and it shouldn't take long to get a sense of how to achieve a handsome, coordinated look.

If you are not comfortable with a jazzy square you can always fall back on a white conservative square—just dress it up with invention—not folded flat, but with some flair. Patterns can be varied and can include bold polka dot designs, geometrics, flowers or location/travel souvenirs. Weddings are a different story, as they call for more subtlety and refinement. Inject your square with character and individuality in order to make your own personal statement about confidence with some adventuresome choices. Evel Knievel's famous quote, "Where there is little risk, there is little reward," fits here as well!

Most important, have fun with your final choices of pocket squares. What's your mood? What's the event? What are you planning to wear? All have an effect on your personal fashion decisions. The only other ingredient you might consider adding to a jacket is a vintage decorative button—perhaps an advertising pin, a saying—"1000 Moose for Norfolk" was my chosen favorite for years. If you are out searching for hanks, don't overlook a small, pinned disc on your lapel. If you have the room in your closet or dresser, consider a little shrine to your collection with convenient containers for hanks, perhaps some hats stacked up and a clear glass container for easy selection of a button for the night. Nearby should be your necktie and bowtie inventory—all properly displayed for enjoyment and inspiration.

ILANDER'S HANKIES *Gallery owner and artist Bruce Helander's collection of pocket squares is large enough to cover him — and his dog Smudgie — from head to toe.*

From a feature article on Palm Beachers' eccentric clothing collections, *Palm Beach Daily News*, May 24, 1994. Photograph by Sig Bokalders.

Perfect Placement and Folding a Hank

by Bruce Helander

The most important aspect of this book, even more than as a means to display part of my collection, its history and helpful practicality, is to offer a perspective on the advantages of utilizing a pocket square and advice for properly folding a printed piece of cloth into a slim horizontal sliver and tucking it into a jacket's breast pocket. Although the pocket square is probably the smallest component in your wardrobe, it also can be the most important singular decision in terms of attention to detail and individual style. Which cloth accessory to wear should be the very last fashion decision made after choosing the main components of your outfit, whether it's just a sports jacket without a tie or my personal favorite, a snappy Brooks Brothers seersucker suit complete with suspender buttons.

The priority is to have an ample amount of handsome pocket squares in a drawer to offer aesthetic choices to the wearer that complement an outfit. I have an entire cabinet that holds literally hundreds of hanks, there are even a few that are so threadbare they are no longer practical to wear. But you really don't need hundreds as a baker's dozen should do. Like a painter preparing for a composition, an artist usually needs to spread out dabs of colors so that there is a full range of choices to balance the final composition. The same theory holds true while preparing an ensemble and not overlooking every opportunity for detail. Having only one boring white hanky is a distinct disadvantage for any compatibility or creativity with respect to individual style. Like having a collection of hot socks that recent technology has allowed designers to weave into delightful designs, such as polka dots or repeat portraits of the family dog or Warhol licensed flowers exposing a little sock sense, and even clad in a tuxedo the wearer can explore a bit of haberdashery excess that is not overwhelming. It's the *details* that count and a jacket without a hanky is a missed opportunity.

In the beginning, handkerchiefs originally were used for hygiene, but with the evolving demands of fashion and originality a simple square that could be tucked or folded for fashion dic the

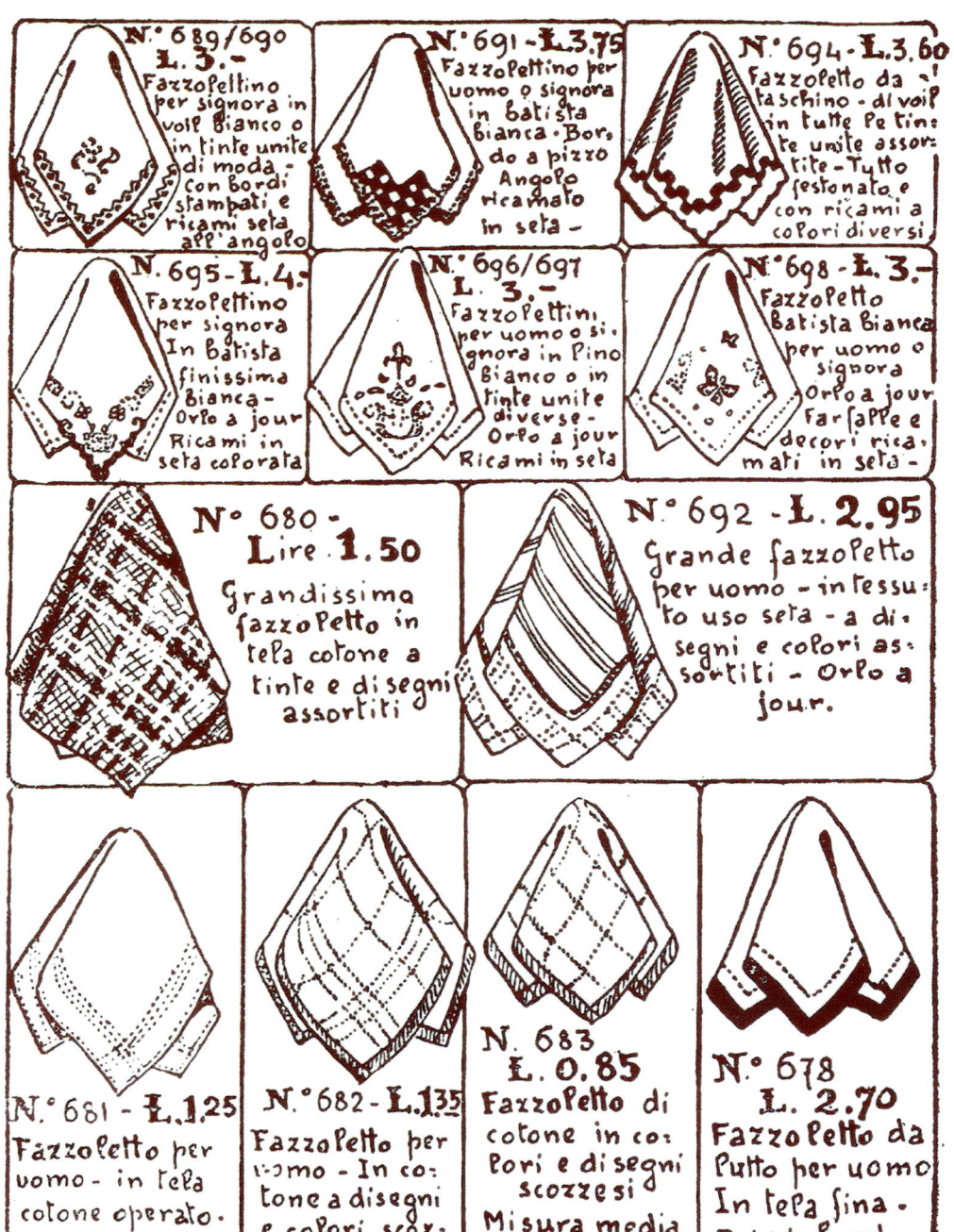

This illustration is from an Italian catalog published in 1910, which showed a range of cotton handkerchiefs in various designs.

job. By the end of the Renaissance, these "little clothes" were commonplace throughout Western Europe and becoming increasingly ornate. Fashion icon Marie Antoinette grew exasperated at the number of shapes and complained to her husband, King Louis XVI of France. He then decreed that all handkerchiefs must have four sides of equal length, and they have remained square ever since.

At first, handkerchiefs were apparently kept in trouser pockets. But as three- and two-piece suits became a trend, jackets were cut with a left breast pocket, allowing hankies to be shown. Soon after, the specific look of a handkerchief became prevalent, and folding techniques came into their own. So, for one reason or another we are blessed with at least the universality of a square shape that really does simplify a practicality of purpose, which also can come across as a work of art. Eventually the pocket square and its fold permitted a sartorial opportunity for self-expression, which continues to this day.

Heaven knows there are as many ways to fold a pocket square as there are fabrics and designs from which to choose. If I have persuaded you to start utilizing the potential magic of a cloth square your first step should be to build a modest inventory of pocket hankies. If you are someone with a certain design discrimination, then you no doubt will be concerned about the physical appearance of your cloth square. Department stores offer distressingly sad designs, so stay away. You can either choose a "Rooms to Go" philosophy where others can decide for you what works or show some independence. The latter requires a bit of creative effort. The best personal attempt is to forage for yourself in secondhand stores or at a Sunday flea market, where your chances of discovering a truly rare square are quite good and the cost may only be a few dollars as opposed to a hundred dollars or more for mass-produced merchandise.

Once you have a variety of inventive and appealing choices for your jacket collection it all comes down to the fold, baby. You can forget what the original design looked like flat or the printed message, as you only need to be aware of the EDGES that will appear in your own personally assembled composition. Don't be distracted by the overall design, such as a flower motif or a Western theme, like composing a picture, it's the little fragment that shows that's important. There are no rules in folding if you feel comfortable preparing your very own arrangement, just go with your instincts.

In my research for this book, I discovered a publication that was dedicated solely to recommending the various options for tucking hanky material into a suit pocket. In fact, the British publisher Thames & Hudson listed twenty-two "essential folds" as suggested choices. The only problem is, in my opinion, none of the folds are very useful; the offered alternatives are pretentious, overworked, ostentatious, poorly designed or completely unnecessary. There were titles to the folds, such as The Presidential, The Peak, The Two Point, The Tulip, The Four Point, The Cagney (which looks like a king's crown and is dismal), Le Croissant, The Tailfin, The Fred Astaire, The Dunaway and The Vesper. I cannot endorse any of these folds, instead, I propose that you reach into your artistic consciousness and craft your own simple fold, which does not have a rule or guideline to be fancy or ingenious but will present a unique design that is naturally compatible with your intuitive vision.

Here's how to practice: Take your favorite hank and spread it out on a table. Take your thumb and forefinger and pull up the material from the exact center of the square. Then, holding it in the air, give it a gentle shake, turning the hank upside down and rotate the original center puff upwards to cover a bit of the edges and gently tuck into your breast pocket. Then check the look in a mirror with a smile and adjust the material into a small utilitarian shape, and *voila*, you have a respectable and inventive silhouette that is all your own!

I recommend cotton or linen cloth for folding. A silk handkerchief has no body or spine and allows no chance to form an interesting placement. Silk material is droopy, shiny and showy, and often is limited to one color, no design, with perhaps some sewn edges. Silk doesn't stand up as its texture is smooth and uninteresting. The ideal measurement for a pocket square is nine- or ten-inches square. Any material much larger than ten or eleven inches becomes too bulky when you try to stuff most of it into a small breast pocket. There should not be a bulging lump under the pocket, just smooth sailing. Some companies try to push a larger size so that you feel you are getting more for your money but it's a counterproductive marketing attempt. In this case, size matters, but ironically, the smaller the better.

I've been folding pocket squares with a smile for forty years, as you never know exactly what your results will be—it is part of the fun of getting dressed. I don't put much time into deliberating or composing, so don't overthink or over-style your placement. Try to keep in mind that you are the artist/creative director—the pile of hanks is your palette—and whatever you come up with that passes your aesthetic artist/stylist test is A-OK. Again, it is the exposed edges that make a great design statement. The center printed illustration only can be successful and not overbearing if it is used sparingly. When adding this last comparatively small necessary accessory be sure that the square has been gently ironed, so that it has a fresh, crisp visual aroma and is not a worn-out square of wrinkled cotton.

Photograph by Tyler Sargent.

Pocket squares, especially secondhand and vintage, should have an honorable resting place in your dressing room. A perfect receptacle is a vintage wooden spool thread box with numerous shallow drawers. I put favorites in the top drawers but never separate according to design or shape. If you can't find something that enhances your stash and is practical at the same time you can always employ a top drawer to save the day. Avoid throwing your collection in an open basket. Show your handkerchiefs some respect. Occasionally, you may want to send your pocket squares to a dry cleaner after numerous nights on the town—but avoid the washing machine!

If you need a better animated visual tutorial, go to: www.magicinasquare.com to see me in action for a demonstration as well as a clip by the renowned Mio the Magician with another interpretation of the Magic in a Square.

A Hankering

by Bruce Helander

Authors write interesting books on a variety of topics, hoping to use their words and occasionally images to prompt a variety of reactions, such as passion, revelation, recollection, nostalgia, addiction, or love, as well as a peculiar editorial individuality that brings an unexpected but enjoyable perspective to their readers. The premise of this book is to celebrate successfully all of the above.

My own perpetual subtle compulsion to collect cloth materials and objects started during my early days as a student at the Rhode Island School of Design. I was introduced to the joys of rummaging through flea markets and secondhand stores by my fellow RISD student, glass artist Dale Chihuly. He was obsessive about eccentric utilitarian items and had an intuitive and sharp eye for discovery. He advised me to look for things that seemed to have an innate personal attraction for acquisition, no matter what their theme. This memorable tip gave me the freedom to expand my interests into collecting anything that expressed both a distinctive visual essence and a practicality—such as pocket squares—and at the same time inspired my admiration and curiosity to procure more.

It only took a few visits and I was hooked. My limited budget as an art student included forays to New England area flea markets and secondhand stores, and it didn't take me long to decide to pursue stuff that had a unique common denominator. I loved collecting things I could wear, such as vintage bowling shirts or handkerchiefs. It's been said that if you acquire two of any subject you have the basis for an engaging compilation, and that is what happened to me. Remarkably, fifty years later, one of my most recent books, *Chihuly: An Artist Collects* (Abrams, Inc., now in its second printing), would examine the commitment, passion and ingenuity that place Dale Chihuly as one of the top artist-collectors of objects in the world, on a par with Andy Warhol and the early history of his collecting habits. It's also fascinating to note that artist Hunt Slonem, whose recent book *Bunnies* (Glitterati Press) I also wrote, is another voracious champion collector like Chihuly. He certainly considers his massive inventory of thousands of objects, sculptures and vintage furniture that now are scattered in several mansions, southern estates and even an historic armory in Scranton as important to his life as his own paintings. Like legendary art collectors, this passion is a lifetime mission that is never-ending.

While you might expect to see fashion icons such as Ralph Lauren or Calvin Klein regularly sporting a pocket square, there are numerous stylish individuals who are not designers or artists that also regularly dress up a sport coat with a snazzy square. Famed photographer Harry Benson always wears the same modest light green silk puff of a hank whenever he ventures out. Remarkably, this constancy has become a natty, iconic look for Benson. Somewhat ironically, Andy Warhol, who revolutionized contemporary art and individual style, preferred wearing jeans, a plain blue jacket with no handkerchief (he prioritized the breast pocket to store several Sharpies for autographs), welfare glasses and an exaggerated white wig. He wasn't much of a dresser but as the most recognizable man in Manhattan, he was remarkably consistent as he set about to create his own simple idiosyncratic ensemble. Apparently, when Andy received his first big check for his *Vogue* magazine shoe illustrations, he bought 100 button-down white shirts from Brooks Brothers, knowing instinctively that he would only be wearing these white shirts for a lifetime. So, a great look and steadfastness of daily style doesn't have to be complicated, just harmonious and balanced, no matter how simple.

Helander's mother, Carmen, was a dancer, designer and eccentric dresser who majored in apparel at the Rhode Island School of Design. She also was an accomplished seamstress and hat maker, and provided an early guiding creative influence on her son.

Even though I intuitively started amassing odd things in grade school with the encouragement of a supportive mother, such as restaurant menus, buttons, quirky tobacco tins and scraps of interesting paper and fabric, I never thought of myself as a bona fide collector but rather a gatherer of bits and pieces with a quirky flair that I could not explain at the time. Eventually, while trying to survive high school with severe dyslexia, collecting became the focus of my activities, and between needing more time and money serious future acquisitions would have to wait.

The evolution of my collecting pursuits began an ongoing and regular passion for gathering unusual objects with a similar design flavor, particularly those with a purpose, including Bakelite radi-

Helander's father, Amos, a Swedish entrepreneur, sign painter and carpenter, regularly enjoyed wearing his collection of hand-painted neckties. Pictured here is Helander's dad, standing under his giant, hand-crafted good luck horseshoe-shaped entrance to their Kansas home.

os, 1950s lamps, salt and pepper shakers from the 1940s (800 pairs), bolts of material and antique wallpaper (especially uncommon paper borders), twig furniture, children's toy stoves, vintage posters and magazines, advertising signs in both enamel and cardboard, tramp art, naïve paintings, Mexican cabinets and more, all of which subliminally infiltrated and stimulated my own work as a budding collage artist and illustrator.

My wife Claudia, a professional garden designer, has shared a similar passion with me for the past twenty-five years for collecting art and antiques that have an inherent aesthetic. We always have outfitted our homes with wonderous objects, and for us our quality of life improved immeasurably by living with (and often wearing) what treasures we had unearthed. One of the collections, vintage handkerchiefs, not only became cherished by me as a confessed man of habitual eccentric style but it turned into a deliberate quest to accumulate hundreds of hanks, which often we would spend time looking through late in the afternoon when we returned home from work, sort of like spreading out all the candy after an evening of trick or treating! Part of the excitement of collecting pocket squares was occasionally finding a shoebox full of someone else's horde of hanks, most always ironed and thoughtfully folded, which we had bought without really investigating what we had purchased. I would set aside my favorites that might incorporate an ideal classic design and wear them proudly tucked into my coat pocket at events and art openings. I also have a selection of colorful bowler hats, often from magic supply stores, which often are companions to my hanks. At the same time, I developed an attraction for vintage bowties and neckties that was impelled by my father's daily ritual of wearing a handsome hand-painted tie. As I grew older, I became more serious and passionate and discriminating about everything around me, realizing that whatever I lived with should have a distinctive edge, from a chair to napkin rings to dinner plates, never to be replaced and enjoyed daily.

When you are a true collector, you don't stop collecting. Availability of space no longer matters. It's the continued search for something rare and inspiring that keeps pushing you to get up

Bruce at his grandparents' farm, wearing his cowboy outfit with holster, handkerchief and hat. The young cowboy loved to dress up in outfits, and the original yellow kids' hank was part of the cowboy outfit, saved by Helander's mother Carmen and sent to him thirty years later by her in a birthday card.

and out early on a Sunday morning to explore the unknown riches of a garage sale or drive-in theater flea market, knowing that your chances of a three-hour hunt in the south Florida sun will no doubt result in characteristic detection, acquisition and satisfaction.

The lyrics of David Byrne, famed musician, founder of the Talking Heads and a former classmate at RISD, specifically "How did I get here?" motivated me to look back at how and why I developed into an artist who fervently collects. If I am to choose my primary mentors that were first and foremost, it would be my talented, far-sighted mother who had attended RISD as a fashion major, and my father, who was an eclectic dresser. The combination of a style conscious Dad and an eccentric stylist Mom offered their son the budding artist the encouragement to pursue his own atypical interests. As I was born in Great Bend, Kansas, where the chances of assimilating and appreciating extraordinary style were less than ideal, and as parental reinforcement is the key to developing an eye for and support of aesthetic sight, I am grateful that my circumstances as a child were wisely nurtured.

So, it was with a bit of irony but no surprise that I followed my mother's motivation and advice and ended up attending RISD, her alma mater and one of America's leading art schools in charming Providence as a midwestern transplant who was as green and naïve as an unsophisticated young schoolboy could be.

Attending the Rhode Island School of Design certainly changed my life with an energized vision and the day-to-day influence of a gifted and determined student body. After receiving a master's degree in fine arts, I achieved my life's ambition to work for *The New Yorker* magazine and later created necktie and shirt designs for fashion designer and former classmate Nicole Miller. In the past forty years I have directed eponymous art galleries in Palm Beach and New York (with a different hank every day) and was Editor-in-Chief of *The Art Economist* as well as a frequent contributor to *The Huffington Post*.

Bruce with Henry Geldzahler, outside Helander's historic Palm Beach cottage on Root Trail.

I was very fortunate to interest the late great Henry Geldzahler to my work. Henry wrote the foreword to my first book, *Curious Collage*, published by Bonnie Clearwater through Grassfield Press. He was Commissioner of Cultural Affairs in New York for five years, a former curator of American art for The Metropolitan Museum of Art and a board member of the Warhol Foundation and possessed inimitable personal style. A close friendship developed. Henry would stay at my home in Palm Beach for a few months during the winter. David Hockney would call my house nearly every morning from L.A. to say hello to his great pal. It always was a pleasure to see him socially in Manhattan. Unfortunately, Henry became ill and passed away long before his time in his Southampton home. When I traveled to the Hamptons to offer my condolences his longtime assistant announced that Henry had provided in his will for me to acquire all his handmade silk bowties, some handkerchiefs, and many eccentric hats from his world travels, all of which I accepted and wore with enthusiasm. The Keith Haring handmade pillbox hat that the artist made for Henry was the greatest surprise! So, often, I come across a handkerchief that Henry gave me that I wear to an occasion with pride and fond memories.

THE REAL THING

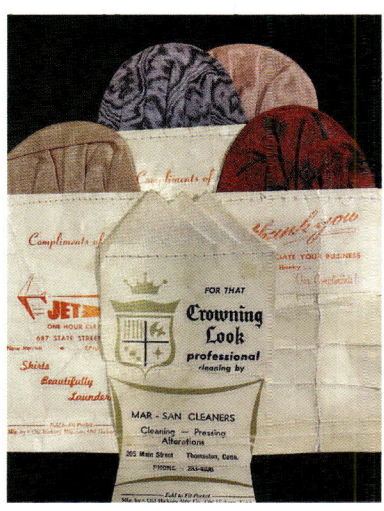

Complimentary dry cleaning advertising cardboard backed pre-made hanks, circa 1950s.

In everything you wear or stylishly create, make sure it's the real thing and not what's called "ready to wear," which doesn't make the effort to generate, as Tom Wolfe would say, The Right Stuff. A starched button-down shirt collar that stands alone is the only exception.

For example, never attempt to place a 'clip-on' bowtie that's pre-knotted and sewn together then attached to your shirt with those terrible unsightly metal clips. It's okay for a kid attending Sunday School but like tying your shoe, knotting the bowtie yourself only needs a little practice to make originality worthwhile. Wearing a ready-made bowtie looks lazy when it just takes another thirty seconds to craft your own original shape into a handsome bowtie. Once you get the hang of hand-constructing a double-sided bowtie you'll never go back to pre-assembled. Bowties are a delightful addition to your wardrobe, especially if you can utilize some great vintage designs and spend a little time mastering a rather simple basic knot and then match it with a snappy hank.

After decades of foraging about in a search and rescue operation for great pocket squares, I did on occasion discover another type of premade handkerchief that was "compliments of one-hour cleaners," which typically was a sad little piece of material often shaped like a setting sun that was sewn into a thin cardboard and placed into your freshly dry-cleaned jacket's breast pocket. The card usually had some advertising and a reminder of an address and telephone number to help SPruce 7-0742 you up. The rare hanky squares "fit to fold" seem amusing and are basically worthless, but now a unique find as they were made to be disposable. These four examples pictured above should be looked at but forgotten.

So, just like everything else in life, if you strive for perfection in what you wear, with particular attention to the details, such as a hank, you can fashion your own unique style using common sense and intuitive foresight, and you'll be well on your way to an unofficial best-dressed list—good hunting!

Hanky Panky
The Language of Pocket Cloths: Lost, But not Forgotten. Ripe for Revival?

by Anthony Haden-Guest

Clothing became a language early. How individuals chose to wrap themselves could indicate tribal identity, signal class differences or intellectual aspirations, show off physical attractions, or simply parade the wearer's taste. The handkerchief would prove peculiarly fit for all these purposes, being of a size to be either covert, discreet, or up-front showy. The first such multi-purpose piece of cloth to get a name appeared in Rome in the time of Cicero, immediately before the emperors, which was when fine linen came into use. The cloth was called a sudarium, Latin for sweat cloth. The poet Catullus wrote about sudaria Saetaba, namely Spanish linen, and there are records of sudaria being waved at gladiator events, dropped to start a chariot race, and as always happens with handkerchiefs, they worked their way into history. In the early 16th century, Albrecht Dürer made a woodcut of the sudarium with which Saint Veronica was said to have washed the face of Christ on his way to the cross, thereby imprinting his image on it.

It was in this period also that Shakespeare used such an intimate cloth to devastating effect in *Othello*. Iago, enraged about not being promoted, revenges himself upon Othello, his general, by seeding suspicions that his young wife, Desdemona, is being unfaithful with the soldier, Cassio. Iago begs his own wife, Emilia, to get him the cloth Othello gave Desdemona. She does so:

I am glad I have found this napkin,
This was her first remembrance from the Moor.
My wayward husband hath a hundred times
Wooed me to steal it, but she so loves the token
(For he conjured her she should ever keep it)
That she reserves it evermore about her
To kiss and talk to. I'll have the work ta'en out
And give 't to Iago. What he will do with it

What Iago did was further poison the mind of Othello. And what Othello does is kill: Desdemona first, then himself.

Othello, the play, is said to have popularized the use of the face cloth. At any rate, for whatever reason, the cloths became fashionable in France, where they were called couvre-chef, or headwear. When the fashion hit Britain, they were called kerchiefs at first, but as folk took to hand-carrying them, to distinguish the cloths for wiping sweat and general cleaning up from those worn on the head, the word 'handkerchief' was born. The British monarchs were recorded as having had a number of handkerchiefs—usually not so many—and those of Elizabeth I were particularly impressive.

Thus, handkerchiefs already had a colorful past as the art of tailoring developed in directions that would allow it to blossom into the item as we know it today. It also was much under the watch of the manners police. Lord Chesterfield, the 18th century arbiter of proper behavior and the author of *Manners makyth Man*, gave plenty of page space to his bugbear, the Awkward Man. *Besides all this he has strange tricks and gestures,* he wrote. *Such as snuffing up his nose, making faces, putting his fingers in his nose, or blowing it and looking afterwards in his handkerchief, so as to make the company sick.*

The physical format of the handkerchief continued to develop in spite of its functional ambiguities. In 1784, King Louis XVI of France, at the urging of Marie Antoinette, decreed that all handkerchiefs should be square. Five years later came the French Revolution but square they mostly have remained, and in the next generation they got a significant boost when lace hankies were sported by Britain's reigning dandy, Beau Brummell. The next major surge was during the 1920s, with usage climbing upwards after they had been planted in what has been their dominant perch ever since: The male breast pocket. *Esquire's Encyclopedia of 20th-Century Men's Fashions observes that As worn by more stylish dressers, they harmonized with the wearer's tie but did not match it in fabric or color.*

So ubiquitous, so much a part of everyday life has the handkerchief been in the 18th, 19th and

20th centuries that it has accumulated a thick treasury of literary uses. There is a key handkerchief scene in *Tristram Shandy* by Laurence Sterne, a nine-volume novel, the first two of which were published in 1759, and which is one of the earliest novels in the English language. The scene elicited a painting by Angelica Kauffman, the Swiss artist, probably the best-known 18th century female artist, in which the attention of both a man and a woman is centered on, yes, the handkerchief.

There are crucial handkerchief scenes in Charles Dickens' widely known novel, *Oliver Twist*, mostly involving Fagin's gang of young pickpockets. Handkerchiefs, so far as young Oliver was concerned, were "articles of luxury" that "had been, for all future times and ages, removed from the noses of paupers . . ." That made them a target of the juveniles, followers of the Artful Dodger, and one hanky theft—for which the innocent Oliver was blamed—was illustrated by George Cruikshank, the great illustrator. So, there's a promising art element working here too.

Hankies are a central part of the life of most children, of course, useful for fun and games such as Pin the Tail on the Donkey and Blind Man's Bluff, as well as helpful for messes, sneezes and tears, so inevitably they have been frequently referenced in children's books, as when Tweedledum and Tweedledee conclude their reading of The Walrus and the Carpenter to Alice in *Through the Looking Glass*.

'I weep for you,' the Walrus said;
'I deeply sympathize.'
With sobs and tears he sorted out
Those of the largest size,
Holding his pocket handkerchief
Before his streaming eyes.

'O Oysters,' said the Carpenter,
You've had a pleasant run!
Shall we be trotting home again?'
But answer came there none—
And this was scarcely odd, because
They'd eaten every one.

The Tale of Mrs Tiggy-Winkle by Beatrix Potter, an early 20th century classic, begins "*Once upon a time there was a little girl called Lucie, who lived at a farm called Little-town. She was a good little girl—only she was always losing her pocket-handkerchiefs!*

Here is E. Nesbit, another early 20th century great, in The Railway Children: *So, when the Green Dragon tore shrieking out of the mouth of its dark lair, which was the tunnel, all three children stood on the railing and waved their pocket-handkerchiefs without stopping to think whether they were clean handkerchiefs or the reverse. They were, as a matter of fact, very much the reverse.* (The Green Dragon was a train.)

In The Hobbit, Bilbo Baggins sneezes and demands that their quest stop until he gets a handkerchief. *You will have to do without pocket handkerchiefs, and a great many other things, before we reach our journey's end, Bilbo Baggins*, says the stern trail boss, the wizard Gandalf.

So, Shakespeare, Dickens, Lewis Carroll, even Tolkien, used handkerchiefs to heighten drama. No accident. Handkerchiefs are handy for concealment as well as display, so magicians have always been big on them, and not just magicians. "A genuine blackguard is never without a pocket-handkerchief," Edgar Allen Poe wrote urbanely in 1845. Bandits wear them to hold up banks. And lawful folk, such as you and I? We have been, it seems, as likely to put handkerchiefs to covert use as bandits and magicians.

Dropping a hanky, a seemingly innocent plea for help back when complex skirts made bending over arduous, has been a 'let's get to know each other' move forever. And the exchange of handkerchiefs has frequently been a precursor to an engagement ring. But the coding gets way knottier and more hard-core than that.

"Handkerchiefs were the smartphones of Victorian London," wrote Lee Ballentine, a poet, in a piece on the subject published online. "In an era when women could not openly express their feelings in public, handkerchiefs were a kind of code." He notes that men would use opera glasses or pocket binoculars to pick up on such signals as the passing of a handkerchief across the eyes, which was saying 'I'm sorry!' Folding a hanky meant 'We need to talk,' winding it around a forefinger warned 'I am engaged to somebody else, so please keep clear.' Also, draping it on a shoulder for a moment beckoned, 'Follow me!' but that the touching of a forehead with a handkerchief warned 'Careful! We are being watched.' Iago would surely have been in his element with this gallery of whisperers.

Sadly, it will be news to few that the glorious handkerchief culture you see here ain't what it used to be. Yes, you'll see a hanky poking from a breast pocket now and again—from mine, for one—and you'll get encouraging words from the world of fine tailoring, as on February 6, 2020, when *Gentleman's Gazette*, a Minneapolis-based style magazine, put *Top 8 Folds For Gentlemen*, a lay-out of hanky arrangements online. Their eight included the Classic Fold, the Upside-Down Puff Fold and the Angel's Peak Fold.

All valiant stuff, but is the broader hanky culture irrecoverably gone, departed along with the Twist and brimming ashtrays? Not necessarily so. Handkerchiefs are not a shape, slotted into a time period, like the top hat or bellbottoms, nor are they immutably married to a style, like Art Deco. They are just what Louis XVI of France ordered: A square. So, a handkerchief is as blank as a fresh

Vintage Italian travel poster. Waving with hankies is an honored tradition at many events, from parades to political events. It also was a way to get attention, or used as a lover's signal, or a prop to show surrender.

canvas, full of promise, and ready to take any shape that fluent fingers can give it. Meaning that the hanky may rise again, as if caught in an updraft, and no hanky-panky about *that*.

— Anthony Haden-Guest is a British-American writer, reporter, cartoonist and art critic based in New York and London. *Financial Times, The Art Newspaper, Vanity Fair* and *The Daily Beast* are but a few of the notable publications that have carried his byline, and he is the author of *True Colors-The Real Life of the Art World*. He also is the news editor of *Saatchi Online*.

Square-Cuts for Star-Shapes: Celebrities and their Pocket Squares

by Elizabeth Sobieski

Joseph R. Biden became the first candidate in forty years to be decorated with a pocket square when he accepted the nomination for President of the United States of America, although his personal white hanky was in his favored 3-petal or 3-point fold, rather than in the 'presidential' fold favored by so many non-presidents. Not since the equally sharp-dressing Ronald Reagan has an American president pledged his allegiance to the pocket square.

As *GQ* stated in September of 2020, even during the height of the pandemic, "The pocket square isn't dead. In fact, since you last checked, brands like Paul Smith have only been making them doper."

And this explains why in May of 2021, the seven young South Korean members of BTS, the world's biggest boy band, all flashed pocket squares, some in black and some in white, in varying folds, when they introduced their hit "Butter" on *The Late Show with Stephen Colbert*. While CBS' Colbert, unlike his spiffily clad bandleader Jon Batiste, doesn't seem to be much of a pocket square man, his counterpart on NBC's *The Tonight Show*, Jimmy Fallon, actually invented a smartphone case that doubles as a pocket square. Working with J. Crew, Fallon produced the Pocket Dial, a clever means of hiding a clunky phone in a breast pocket by only revealing the handsome fabric of a pocket square. There is a history of pocket square-wear linked to *The Tonight Show*. The legendary and always stylish Johnny Carson was one of the first celebrities to launch an eponymous line of clothing in the 1960s and some vintage Johnny Carson Apparel brand handkerchiefs are still available on eBay.

Contemporary late night host James Corden also has become enamored with pocket squares, especially with his new trimmer silhouette. He recently revealed a most attractive envelope-fold silk square in burgundy paisley.

Celebrities and pocket squares share a long history. Often considered the best dressed men of the first half of the twentieth century, the Duke of Windsor and Fred Astaire rarely appeared suit-

Fred Astaire

Humphrey Bogart

Cary Grant

ably suited without a pocket square. Just after the turn of the twentieth century, the child Astaire already was displaying a nifty handkerchief emerging from a tiny pocket in photographs of him with his longest-serving dance partner, his sister Adele. The dapper duke always favored patterns and colors and was rarely seen without a jaunty pocket square in either a puff or a 1-point fold.

Another impeccably dressed figure from that era was Cary Grant. In a 1962 piece for *This Week* magazine, Grant offered some fashion advice: "If your pocket handkerchief is monogrammed, don't wear it carefully folded to show the monogram peeking above your breast-pocket. That's somehow ostentatious."

James Cagney, the tough guy actor and elegant hoofer, was so noted for his omnipresent pocket squares that there is even a pocket square fold named for him, The Cagney Fold, which basically is a 4-point fold in reverse.

Gary Cooper was a peacock-fold man. David Niven chose the scallop. Winston Churchill sported pocket squares from the time he was a young schoolboy.

The late Duke of Edinburgh, Prince Philip, perhaps everyone's most on-point embodiment of a handsome prince, almost always maintained a neatly folded trademark white handkerchief, made by Savile Row tailors Kent & Haste, in his breast pocket. At his funeral, Queen Elizabeth carried one of them in her handbag, a fibrous symbol of her beloved husband of 73 years.

Their son, Prince Charles, sports a pocket square almost as often as his mother carries her handbag, basically all the time when jacketed. The future king's hankies resemble those of his great uncle, the Duke of Windsor, more so than his father's; they are colorful and patterned, usually silk and from Turnbull & Asser, adding a beguiling puff to his attire.

In the iconic 1942 film *Casablanca*, Humphrey Bogart's Rick wears a white linen pocket square with his white dinner jacket in non-air-conditioned Morocco, and Dooley Wilson plays it again as Sam in a pale satin tuxedo enhanced by a dark plethora-fold pocket square. In his off-screen life, Bogey also was a handkerchief aficionado, actually preferring a peacock-fold.

Another memorable look from the movies is that of Robert De Niro in Martin Scorsese's *Casino*; set in the 1970s, De Niro's Las Vegas habitué wears dozens of fabulous ensembles including a tangerine open-neck shirt beneath a tattersall suit, flashing a puff of taxi yellow pocket square, and on another occasion, his attire features a paler lemon-hued 3-point hank complementing his cherry suit and paired pink tie and shirt. In 1968's *The Thomas Crown Affair*, the dashing fashion icon Steve McQueen, nicknamed "the king of cool," tended towards printed puffs. A more recent "king of cool," Samuel L. Jackson, has been known to wear a purple silk envelope fold with a purple velvet suit. Another notable purple enthusiast, Prince, was a frequent proponent of vivid contrasting pocket squares in various folds.

In Wong Kar-Wai's exquisite Hong Kong set *In the Mood for Love*, star Tony Leung Chiu-wai's character, the always yearning and remarkably handsome Mr. Chow, presents a mesmerizing white pocket square with his charcoal silk shantung suit.

The most notable European style icon of the latter part of the 20th century, billionaire businessman and FIAT heir, Gianni Agnelli, who set a trend by strapping his wristwatches with their crystal faces on the inside of his wrist, often was spotted wearing a simple square-top pocket square, in white or pale blue. His grandson, Lapo Elkann, both a somewhat notorious figure and a member of *Vanity Fair*'s Best Dressed Hall of Fame, inherited his *Nonno*'s sartorial flair although he favors a more complicated handkerchief than his grandfather, either a bouquet-fold or a slope-fold.

All the movie James Bonds, from Connery to Craig, have exhibited rectangular-fold pocket squares in white Sea Island Cotton or linen when formally attired. Turnbull & Asser has even produced a line of colorful handkerchiefs displaying the original 1958 illustrations by artist John McLusky that are based upon author Ian Fleming's vision of Bond.

The late menswear designer John Weitz, something of a James Bond himself, having served as an OSS intelligence officer in Germany during World War II, was one of the first to license his designs. In the 1960s, he licensed a company in Lake Como, Italy, to manufacture silk pocket squares in various patterns.

But while pocket squares adorned the breasts of the world's most debonaire gentlemen for most of the 20th century, they were somewhat of a rarity around the turn of the 21st. During the 1980s and '90s, pocket squares had slipped slowly out of fashion, although such stylish pen-to-paper men as the late Tom Wolfe, the late Sir David Tang and the living Gay Talese continued the pursuit. Talese tends to favor bold patterns on his squares and understated patterns on his ties and refers to pocket squares as "flags of fashion."

But it really took the retro-cool styling of the 1960s-set hit TV series *Mad Men* on AMC to revive the pocket square, which garnered a fashion-forward new audience after its premiere in 2007. Actor Jon Hamm and his co-stars became mad influencers, leading an ongoing renaissance of the pocket square. Hamm's Don Draper wore a flat-fold, John Slattery's Roger Sterling a 3-point, and Robert Morse's Bert Cooper a 4-point fold.

Left: Churchill when he was a young schoolboy at Harrow.
Right: Nearly seventy years later he pauses outside his Hyde Park Gate home with Lady Churchill.
Cover picture: Photographed by Karsh of Ottawa, Sir Winston is seen wearing the Order of Merit. On his left is the Town Crier's bell presented to him by the Trustees of Colonial Williamsburg, as first recipient of the Williamsburg Award, in 1955

Born into wealth, he did more than anyone to preserve the Age of the Common Man. A fearless fighter, he found his greatest pleasures in the pursuits of peace. A life-long

Like most squares, the effect of a Rolled Puff (simply rolling the cloth to create a large 'puff') is common and useful. Sir Winston Churchill wore a huge number of pocket squares with designs and variants to project his image as an orator (think Tom Wolfe). For some of Churchill's most important and stirring speeches he would tease two twisted points from the sides of his Rolled Puff and create a striking "V" for Victory. Clipping courtesy of Edwina Sandys, Churchill Collection, Palm Beach.

Today, young icons of male chic, such as Timothée Chalamet, Robert Pattinson, Rami Malek, Eddie Redmayne, Idris Elba, Ryan Reynolds, Jason Momoa, Nick Cannon, Jonah Hill, Sacha Baron Cohen, Benedict Cumberbatch, Henry Golding, Chris Pine and Donald Glover, often appear at events adorned with handsome hankies. They follow in the footsteps of sensational fellow wearers Jeremy Irons, Brad Pitt, Denzel Washington and Keanu Reeves. The most stellar dresser at the 2021 Oscars was Leslie Odom Jr. in a gold double-breasted Brioni suit coordinated with a gold shirt—and a gold pocket square.

Such handsome contemporary designers as Brunello Cucinelli and Tom Ford, often their own best models, favor pocket squares. Ford sometimes utilizes both a pocket square and a gardenia flower to dress up his jackets. And Cucinelli, the "king of cashmere," tends to incorporate such juxtapositions as a pink polka dotted pocket square with a blue tie.

The most important man in fashion, the man who has overtaken Jeff Bezos as the wealthiest person on earth, billionaire LVMH chairman and chief executive Bernard Arnault, is only an occasional *le mouchoir de poche* wearer, but his two dashing eldest sons often are photographed with *la pochette* emerging from a pocket.

Though now merely the world's second richest man, Bezos (he may resume first position by the time this is published) frequently wears a pocket square, although perhaps not for space travel.

Men in music often play with a pocket square. Both Nat King Cole and Frank Sinatra were regular wearers. Early on, all four Beatles were photographed with pocket handkerchiefs, precursors to the BTS boys. Sean "Diddy" Combs likes to change it up, sometimes donning 3-petals, sometimes a rabbit and sometimes a slope-fold. Kanye West has been spotted with bouquet-folds. The legendarily trend-setting David Bowie was known to wear a red 2-point during the 1970s and returned to hanky form in the twenty-first century when he was promenading with his beauteous wife Iman. Sir Elton John often dons a pocket square, and sometimes even seems to insert two into his breast pocket. Harry Styles, arguably the biggest men's *style(s)* influencer of today, the only man to appear solo on a *Vogue* cover during the magazine's 128-year existence, has been known to exhibit a pocket handkerchief, when not dressed in a dress. The elegant music men, John Legend and Mark Ronson, always look especially natty on red carpets when flashing their hankies.

LeBron James created a fashion frenzy sporting a white presidential fold-embellished gray flannel blazer with a pair of matching shorts, a suit by Thom Browne that he somehow managed to pull off. Trend-setting athletes like James, Henrik Lundqvist, Russell Westbrook, Cristiano Ronaldo, Cam

Frank Sinatra   Nat King Cole

Newton and Tom Brady have all often displayed colorful cloth emerging from their coat pockets. Now retired but seemingly omnipresent, Shaquille O'Neal favors a bright puff and the always-snappy soccer god David Beckham prefers a simple straight fold. And like President Biden, basketball G.O.A.T. Michael Jordan wears a 3-point, and sometimes even a 4-point. (Okay, we do associate Jordan with more points than that.) The late Kobe Bryant preferred a straight fold in muted colors.

Visual artists sometimes showcase their creativity by displaying a jolt of color when not painting, filmmaking, or sculpting. David Hockney, Julian Schnabel, Michael Chow, Taika Waititi and the late Peter Beard all have been pocket square partakers.

Billy Porter is as much renowned for his fashion choices as for his talent. The triple threat Grammy, Tony and Emmy winner wore a black velvet ballgown to the Oscars in 2019. Designed by Christian Siriano, the dress features wide crinoline skirting and a tuxedo top, and what appears to be just a hint of a conservative black satin strip peering from Porter's left breast pocket.

— Elizabeth Sobieski is the author of *The Masked Hatter: Pandemic Style on the Upper West Side* (2021). A novelist and screenwriter as well as a journalist, her profiles of esteemed living artists and interviews with collectors and gallerists graced the cover of *The Art Economist* multiple times. Her journalism career also has included profiling philanthropists, actors, musicians, architects, designers, producers, vintners and car collectors for a variety of publications, including *New York* magazine, *White Hot* magazine, *Avenue* magazine, *New York Post*, *Automobile* magazine, *Cosmopolitan*, *The Huffington Post* and *Medium*.

The Helander Collection

The pages that follow are a colorful presentation of selected designs from my handkerchief collection, separated into six separate favorite categories: geometric designs, polka dots, cowboy/Western themes, travel souvenirs, flower motifs and children's cartoons.

I would like to thank fellow hank collector Barbara Guggenheim for loaning us a few beauties from her extensive assortment and for her encouragement.

There are, of course, numerous categories of other printed thematic images just waiting to be discovered. My interest in amassing a hanky collection that has grown to over 1,000 handkerchiefs began solely with the idea that I would pick something appealing that might be a useful accent to my wardrobe. But if you are a collector of any objects, once you get going it's hard to stop.

Just like a great vintage paper collage fragment, pocket squares that have seen better days still retain a handsome patina called "shabby chic," akin to a great pair of worn-down dress shoes that continue to display an impressive polish.

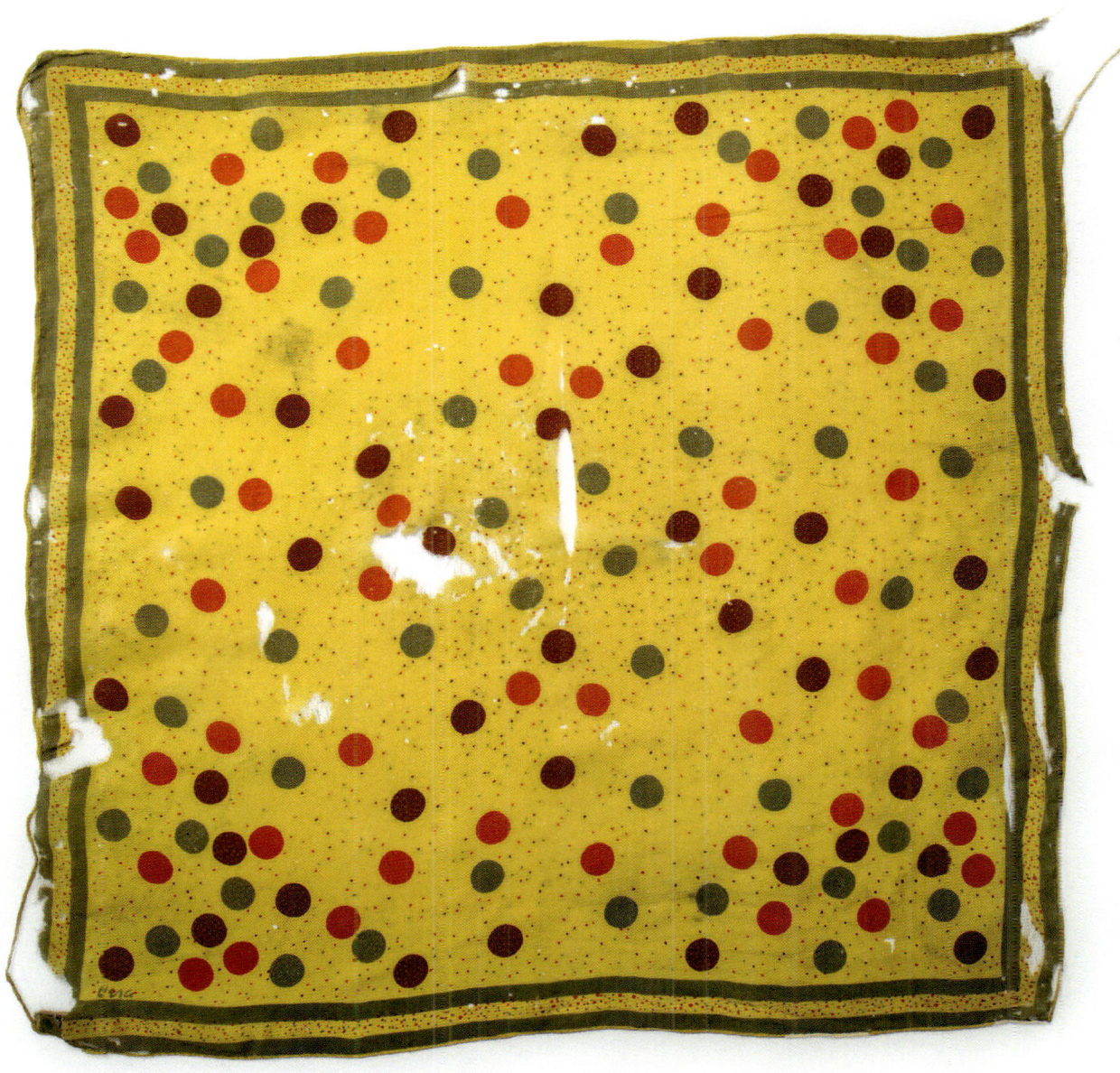

My favorite designs are polka dot varieties and geometric repeat patterns, as they often have the most intriguing edges.

"Pocket handkerchiefs are optional, but I always wear one."
—*Frank Sinatra*

"Style is a simple way of saying complicated things."
—*Jean Cocteau*

"What you wear is how you present yourself to the world, especially today, when human contacts are so quick. Fashion is instant language."
—*Miuccia Prada*

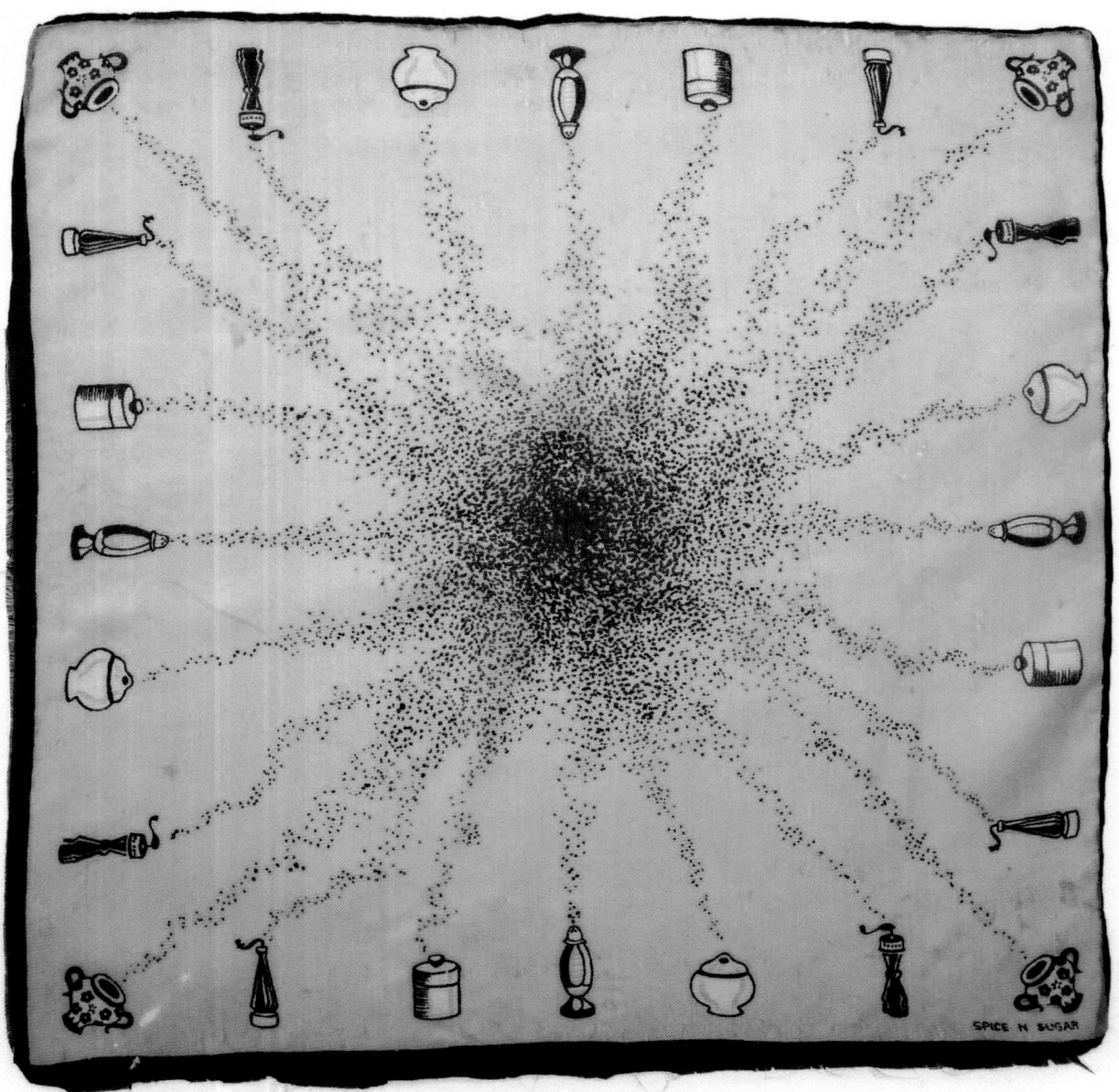

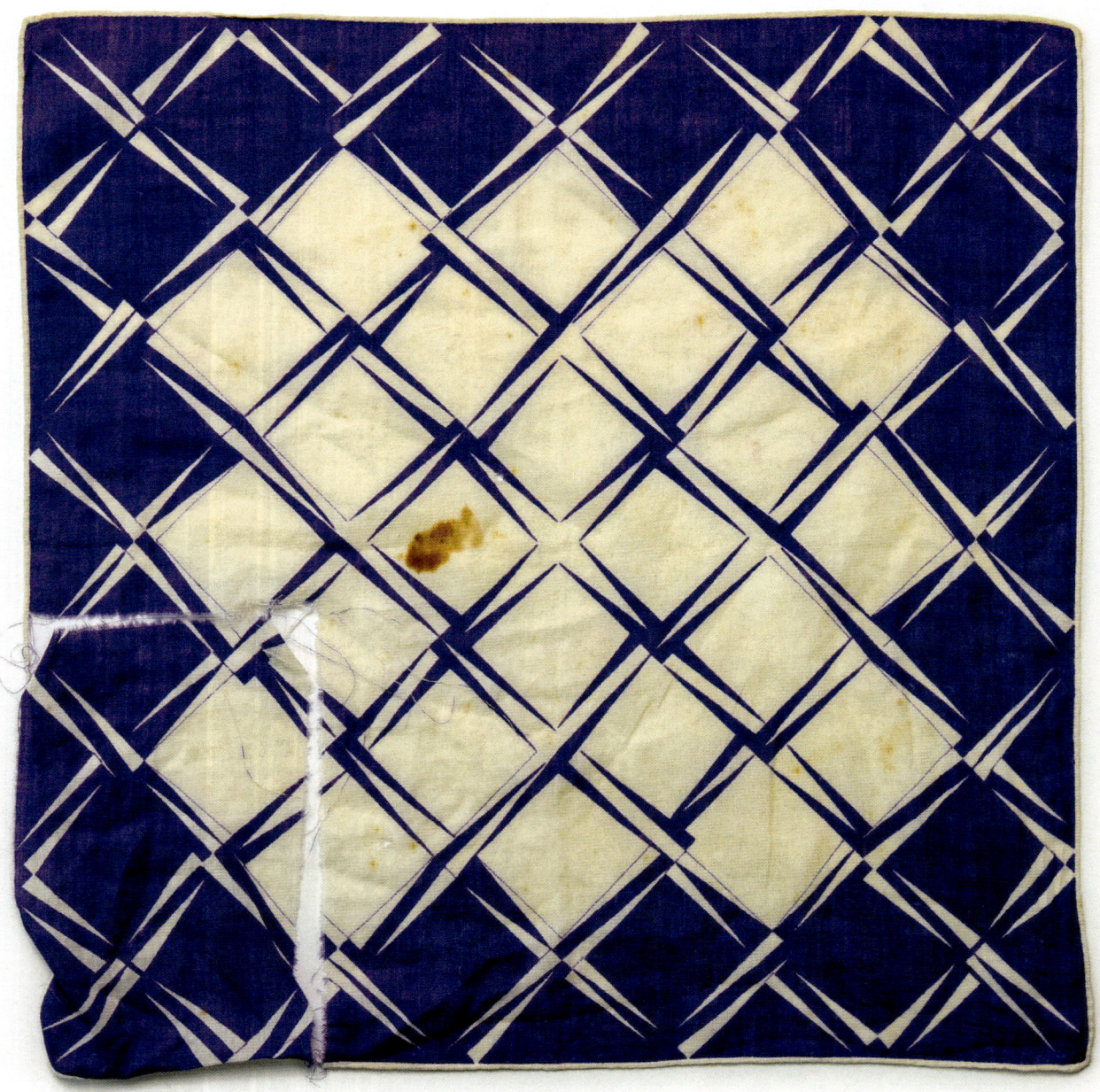

Photographs by Tyler Sargent.

The Wedding Dress

Twenty-five years ago, I met Claudia, my future bride, by chance in Palm Beach. She was from Bogota, Colombia and possessed a remarkable creative aura. It definitely was love at first sight. Our first date was at a Sunday flea market, where soon I realized we had a common appreciation for eccentric objects and collecting in general.

When we decided to get married, the idea of Claudia wearing a traditional wedding gown just didn't fit. So, I suggested that I sew her dress out of my vintage collection of white handkerchiefs. This began a four-week process of having Claudia stand on a coffee table each evening while I pinned selected hanks to a silk body stocking, starting at the hem and working my way up to the neckline. The method was like creating a collage from its foundation with an eye towards interesting white handkerchiefs that often had an embroidered decorative message like Barbados or a "B" (for Bruce), Oddfellows Club and some handsome Art Deco embroidery. The materials were attached on the bias so that each individual square became a symbolic diamond shape.

The photograph here shows the entire dress with some details. The dress also is 'showing its age' by slowly turning a tan color after hanging on display for decades, but dry cleaning it now would be too risky! It remains one of our most prized possessions.

Souvenir travel scarves and handkerchiefs have great edges with a hidden subject folder inside.

There are tons of "informational" hanks out there, offering guidance on subjects from insomnia to snow skiing warnings. Always keep your eyes open for good advice!

Occasionally a square can take on the properties of an artist's canvas. In this grouping, we can connect with hankies reminiscent of Kenneth Noland's circles, Piet Mondrian's squares, Damien Hirst's dots and spots and John Torreano's diamond shapes.

These pocket square images are part of Barbara Guggenheim's extensive collection and were originally published in her book (2004) "Handkerchiefs – A Collectors Guide," Volume II, co-written by Helene Guarnaccia. (Used with permission by the authors)

Don't pass up an old hank due to dubious condition--the tears and worn out spots add to its singular character.

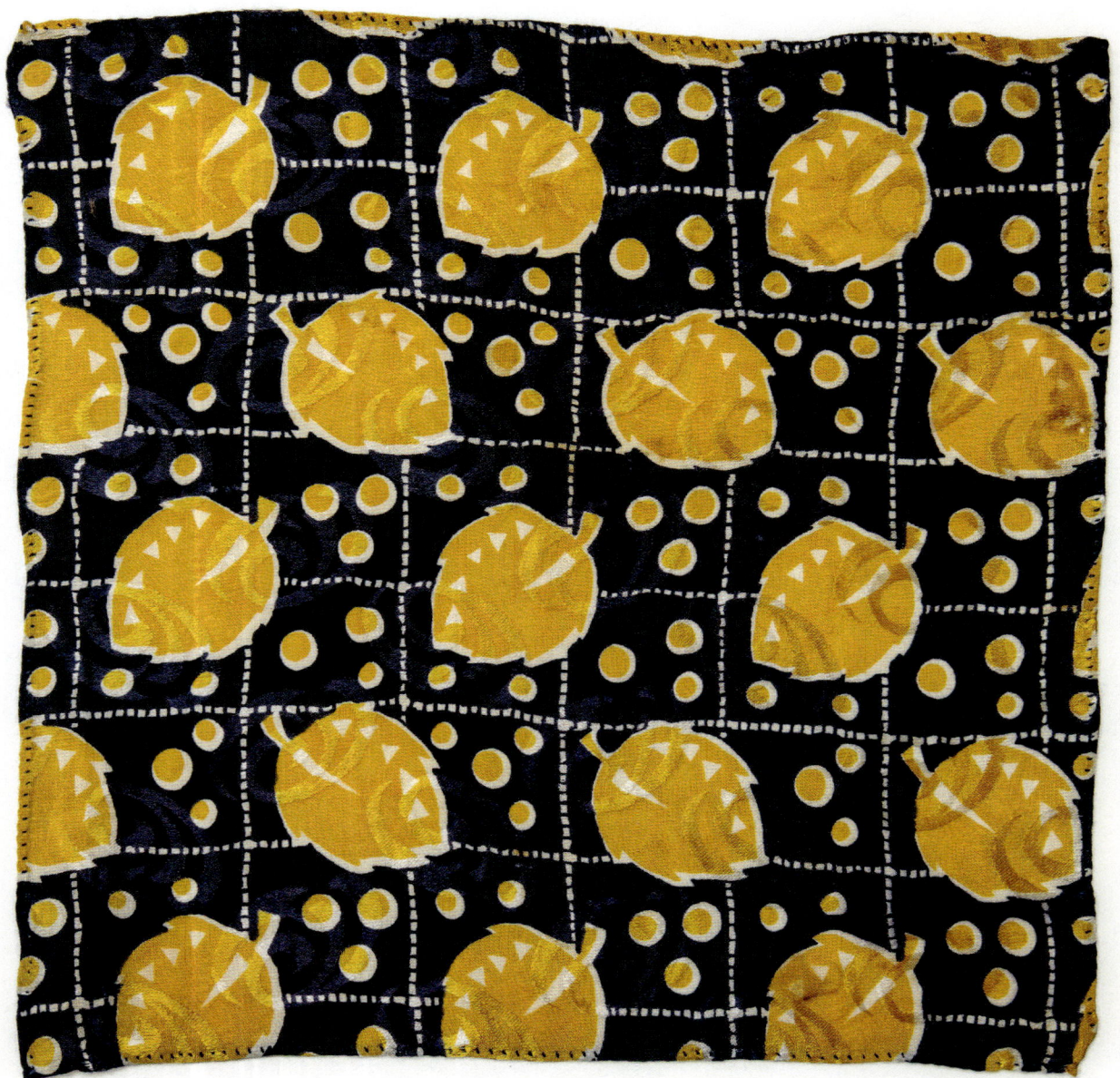

"Fashion is the armor to survive the reality of everyday life."
—Bill Cunningham

*"Fashion is about dressing according to what's fashionable.
Style is more about being yourself."*
—Oscar de la Renta

"The joy of dressing is an art."
—John Galliano

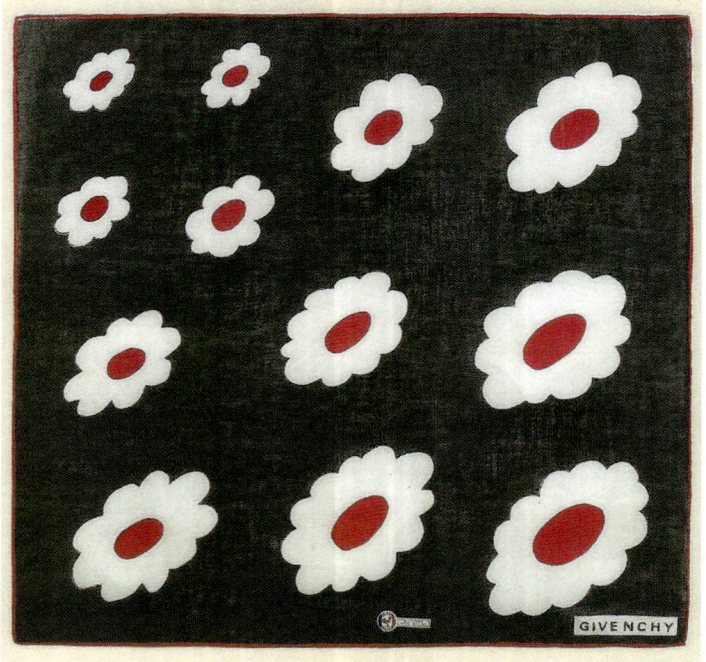 

These pocket square images are part of Barbara Guggenheim's extensive collection and were originally published in her book (2004) "Handkerchiefs – A Collectors Guide," Volume II, co-written by Helene Guarnaccia. (Used with permission by the authors)

Although I usually don't look to match a hank with a holiday (and I certainly could match them all by now), it's fun to secretly wear a thematic square on Easter, or a pumpkin design on Halloween.

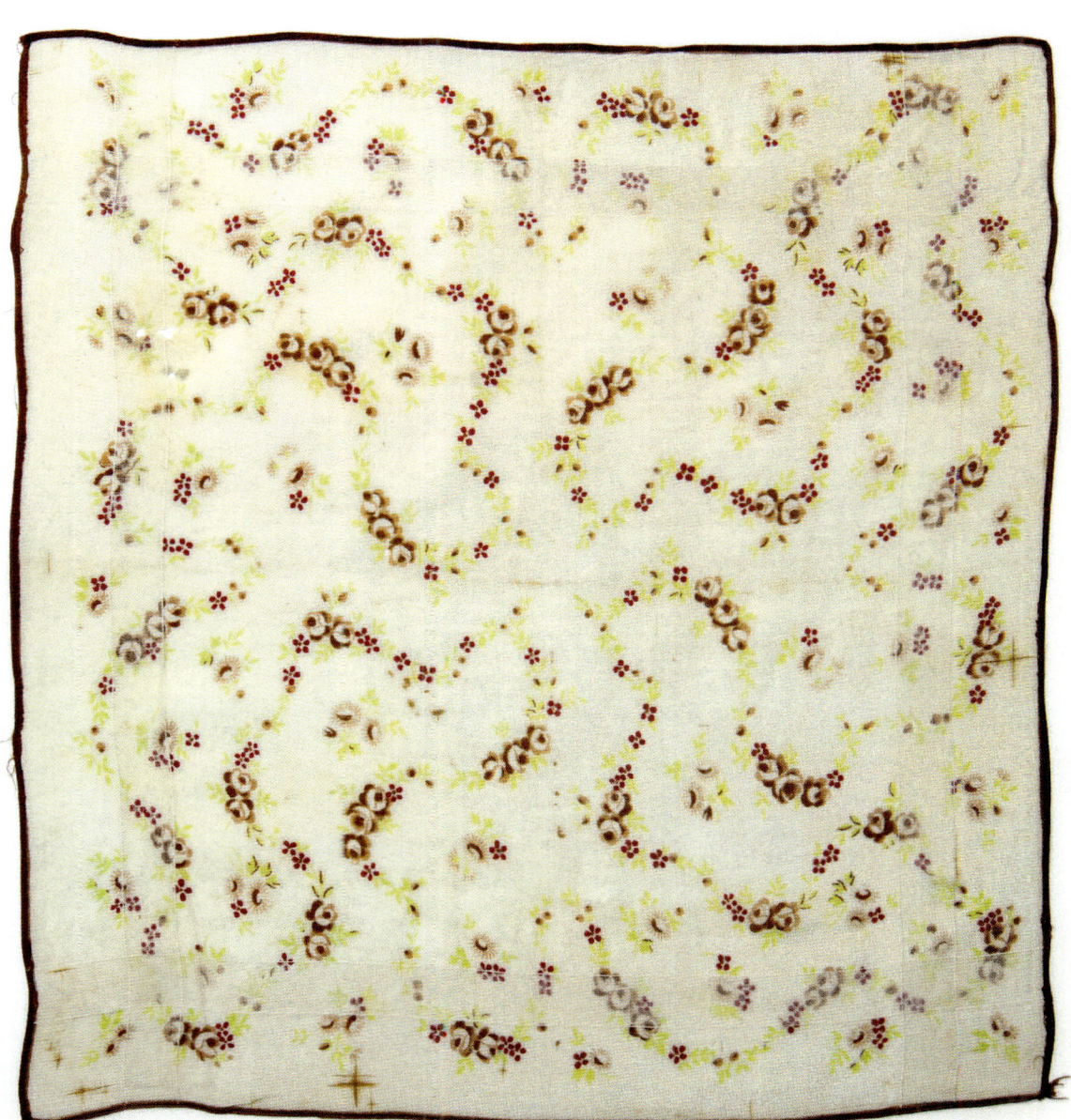

It's easy to see how many of these nine-inch beauties can pass for works of art, especially if they were six-feet square canvases!

When you start looking seriously for great pocket squares, you'll discover lots of western-themed designs, which often are campy and cartoonish, but very useful in a breast pocket with a wooden frame motif peeking out.

*"Style is something each of us already has,
all we need to do is find it."*
—Diane von Furstenberg

*"Don't be into trends. Don't make fashion own you,
but you decide what you are, what you want to express
by the way you dress and the way to live."*
—Gianni Versace

"Dressing well is a form of good manners."
–Tom Ford

Not surprisingly, flowers are the most abundant design subject of collectible cloth squares, as they were perfect for a lady's handbag. Colorful blooms and vines can accentuate the folded edges for an outstanding accompaniment to other garments.

"I think there is beauty in everything.
What 'normal' people perceive as ugly,
I can usually see something of beauty in it."
—Alexander McQueen

"Fashion you can buy, but style you possess.
The key to style is learning who you are, which takes years.
There's no how-to road map to style.
It's about self-expression and, above all, attitude."
—Iris Apfel

"Isn't elegance forgetting what one is wearing?"
—Yves Saint Laurent

These pocket square images are part of Barbara Guggenheim's extensive collection and were originally published in her book (2004) "Handkerchiefs – A Collectors Guide," Volume II, co-written by Helene Guarnaccia. (Used with permission by the authors)

Kids'-related imagery also is one of the easiest to discover at a flea market or secondhand store.
When properly folded, the surface leaves no evidence of a child-themed design--just great corners and edges as seen here.

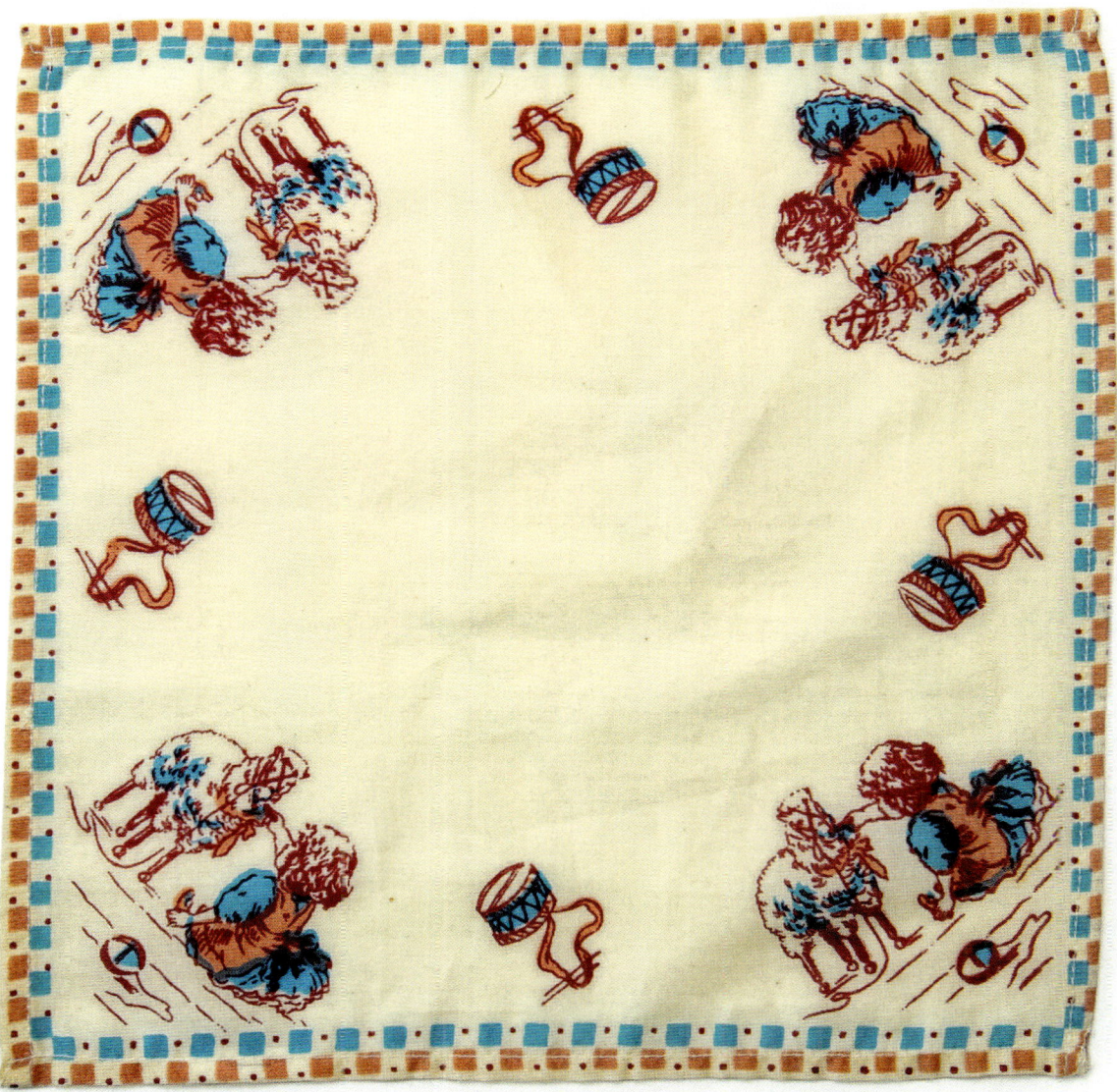

Photographs by Tyler Sargent.

Bedspread

We have a wonderful vintage bedspread made from about one hundred children's hanks circa 1930s that we discovered twenty years ago in mint condition and in the original unopened boxes at a secondhand store. After informing my mother of our great find, she volunteered to sew them all together in the great tradition with quilting material, and to this day it remains on our bed. Pictured here also is our grand-dog, Wilson, posing on the bedspread that covers the turn-of-the-century French farmhouse cast iron bed in our downtown West Palm Beach loft.

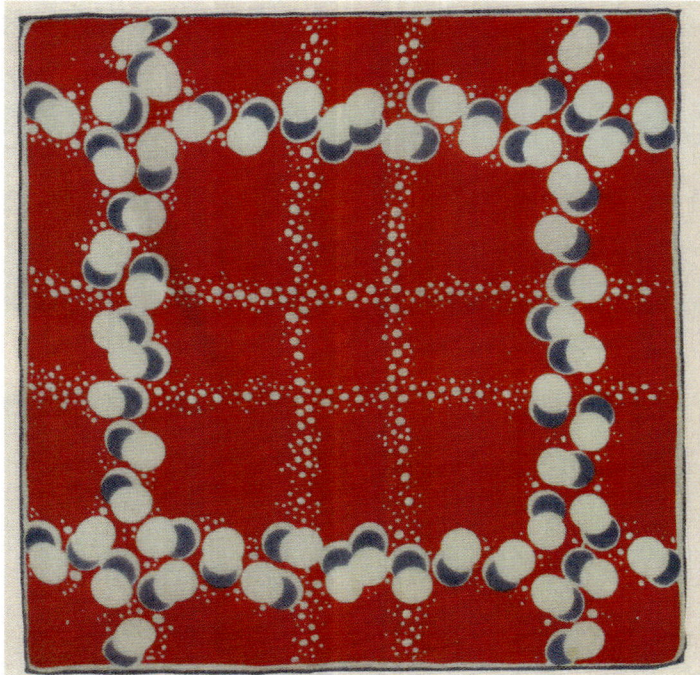

These pocket square images are part of Barbara Guggenheim's extensive collection and were originally published in her book (2004) "Handkerchiefs – A Collectors Guide," Volume II, co-written by Helene Guarnaccia. (Used with permission by the authors)

*"I always find beauty in things that are odd and imperfect,
they are much more interesting."*
—Marc Jacobs

*"A little bad taste is like a nice splash of paprika.
We all need a splash of bad taste—it's hearty, it's healthy, it's physical.
I think we could use more of it. No taste is what I'm against."*
—Diana Vreeland

"Can't repeat the past? Why of course you can!"
–Jay Gatsby

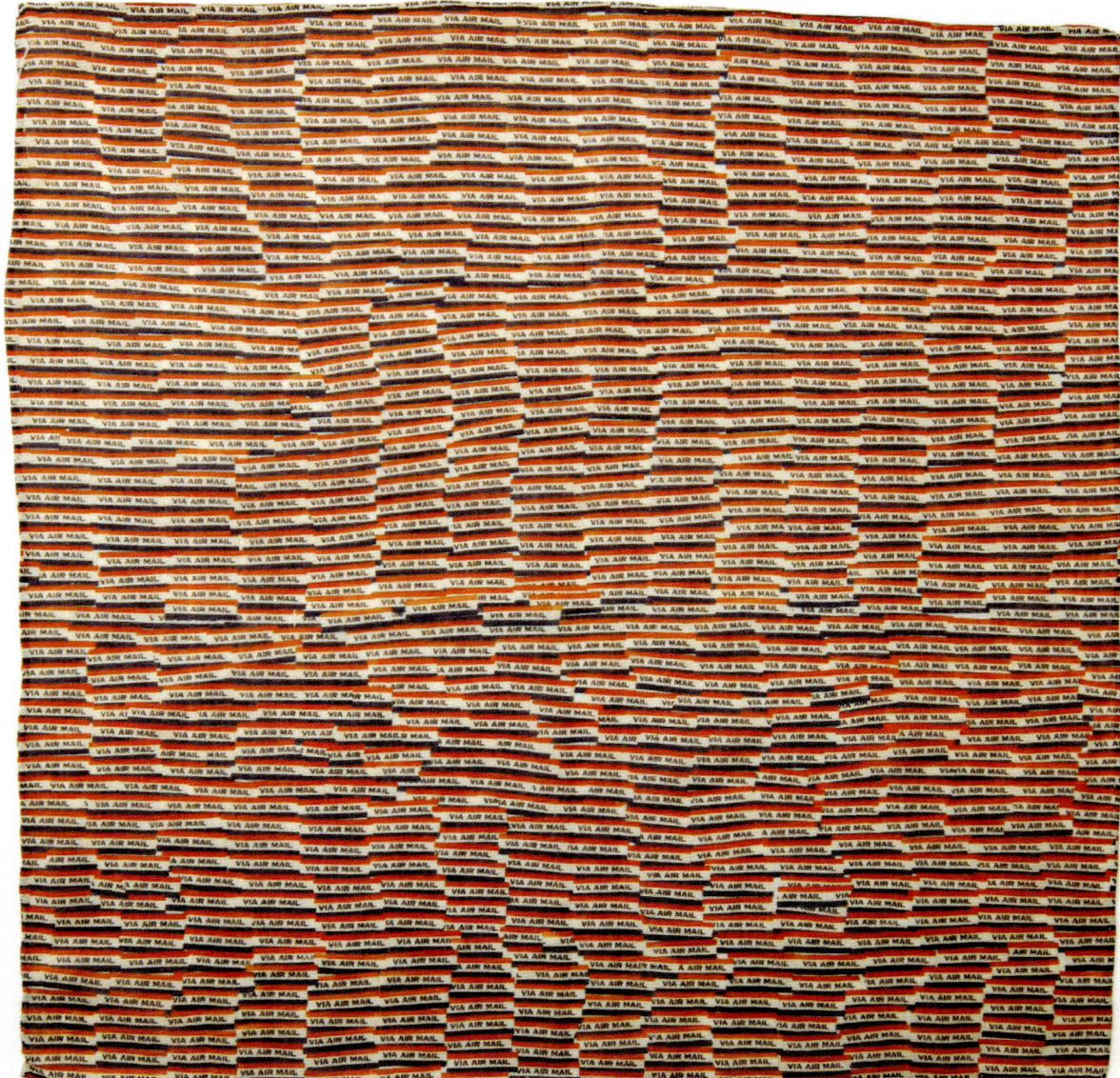

Italo Scanga, the great neo-dadaist/neo-expressionist artist designed these two handkerchiefs as part of a series at The Fabric Workshop, Philadelphia in 1984. Reprinted with permission, the Italo Scanga Foundation, San Francisco.

To view a four-minute "hands-on" studio demonstration video of Helander's suggested formula and easy steps for shaping a perfect pocket square go to: **www.magicinasquare.com**

To watch Mio, the internationally acclaimed magician, weave a remarkable close-up tale of real-life magic in a square utilizing a handkerchief from this book go to: www.magicinasquare.com

We are delighted to support our local independent bookstore. To order copies of "The Magic in a Square," please contact: Classic Bookshop at +1 (561) 655-2485. They are open seven days a week and can take orders and ship daily. If you would like to visit them while in South Florida, they are located at 310 South County Road in Palm Beach, Florida 33480.

Other recent books by Helander may also be ordered through Classic Bookshop: *Chihuly: An Artist Collects* (Abrams, Inc.), *Hunt Slonem - Bunnies* (Glitterati Press, New York), and *Learning to See—An Artist's View on Contemporary Artists from Artschwager to Zakanitch* (StarGroup International).

No portion of this book may be reproduced without permission from the publisher. Brief quotes and illustrations are pre-approved for media reviews and articles. All rights reserved. No part of this book may be reproduced, stored in any retrieval system, or transmitted in any form, or by any means including but not limited to electronic, mechanical, photocopy, recording, or otherwise, without the written consent of the author and publisher.

What we are delivering next....

Helander's collection of vintage bowling shirts! Summer of 2022.